JUST SAYIN'

CAROL McADAMS MOORE

JUST SAYIN'

WRITE 'EM,
DRAW 'EM,
HIDE 'EM
IN YOUR ♥

90
DEVOTIONS

ZONDERKIDZ

Just Sayin'
Copyright © 2014 by Carol Lynn Moore

Requests for information should be addressed to:

Zonderkidz, 3900 Sparks Dr. SE, Grand Rapids, Michigan 49546

ISBN 978-0-310-74298-2

Published in association with the Books & Such Literary Agency, 52 Mission Circle, Suite 122, PMB 170, Santa Rosa, CA 95409-5370, www.booksandsuch.biz.

Cover: Deborah Washburn
Interior design: David Conn
Interior images: Shutterstock, www.istockphoto.com
Printed in the United States of America

14 15 16 17 18 19 20 /DCI/ 22 21 20 19 18 17 16 15 14 13 12 11 10 9 8 7 6 5 4 3 2 1

ENTER
HERE

Read something awesome about God.
Learn something cool about yourself. Then ...

Doodle

Write

Paint

Glue

Whatever

Sweet! Learning to follow Jesus.

Best. Idea. Ever.

1 SERIOUSLY?
LET ME SEE THAT!

The Lord says: "These people come near to me with their mouth and honor me with their lips, but their hearts are far from me. Their worship of me is based on merely human rules they have been taught."

Isaiah 29:13

Spectacular. Idea.

What helps me truly worship God from my heart ...

reading
my Bible

music

time alone
with God
(prayer)

praise

_____ (U name it)

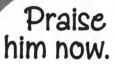

Praise him now.

Doodle a praise pic OR write praise (a poem, a note, or a song).

A time at church when my heart and my lips were not the same ...

SERIOUSLY?
LET ME SEE THAT!

"Enter through the narrow gate. For wide is the gate and broad is the road that leads to destruction, and many enter through it. But small is the gate and narrow the road that leads to life, and only a few find it."

Matthew 7:13–14

What things or people could help you find the way to God's small gate of eternal life? Circle your answers.

the right clothes

my Bible

church

having many friends

a nice house

prayer   cell phone

talking with Christians

following Jesus' example

Spectacular. Idea.

Doodle the way to God's narrow gate. Decorate the gate to make it BEAUTIFUL—glitter, color, sparkle, shimmer ...

What things are on the way?

What things lead away from the gate?

Jesus explained that eternal life is like going through a small gate. Super important. You have to pay attention to where you are going.

SERIOUSLY?
LET ME SEE THAT!

I will give thanks to you, Lord, with all my heart; I will tell of all your wonderful deeds. I will be glad and rejoice in you; I will sing the praises of your name, O Most High.

Psalm 9:1–2

Spectacular Idea.

You are going to be a busy gal. Count all the things to do in Psalm 9:1–2. How will that look? Doodle yourself doing all four.

The verses say that you "will sing the praises of your (God's) name." Write your tune to God under the bars.

4

SERIOUSLY? LET ME SEE THAT!

"This third I will put into the fire; I will refine them like silver and test them like gold. They will call on my name and I will answer them; I will say, 'They are my people,' and they will say, 'The Lord is our God.'"

Zechariah 13:9

Spectacular.Idea.

Doodle the most fab gold and silver bling here (use metallic pens and markers)

Now tell about it:

valuable, beautiful, —————————,

———————, ———————.

Dear God,
Love, love, love bling! I am silver and gold to you? Amazing! That makes me feel
_____. Amen

Yeah. That is Y-O-U in God's eyes. If you are his, you are pure like silver and gold.

5 SERIOUSLY? LET ME SEE THAT!

Then the LORD God said to the woman, "What is this you have done?"

The woman said, "The serpent deceived me, and I ate."

Genesis 3:13

Gulp. **What do you say when you do something wrong? Eve blamed the serpent (think *snake*).**

When I do something wrong, I usually (circle all that are true):

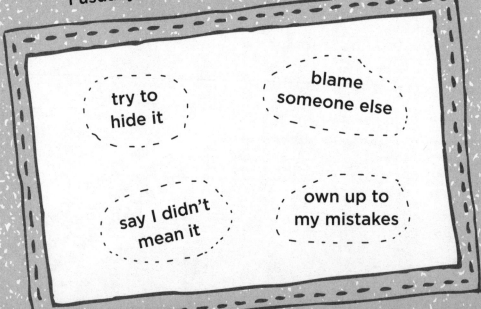

try to hide it

blame someone else

say I didn't mean it

own up to my mistakes

Spectacular. Idea.

Think of a time when you were with your friends and goofed up. (We all have done it.) Which choice did you make that time? Doodle what happened. Doodle what could have happened if you made the other choice.

blamed

owned up

6 SERIOUSLY? LET ME SEE THAT!

"They will be like a well-watered garden, and they will sorrow no more. Then young women will dance and be glad."

Jeremiah 31:12 – 13

Read more about it in Jeremiah 31:7 – 14!

Doodle a garden on this page. Glue on some pressed flowers or garden seeds.

Growing, changing, praising ... what a beautiful life God has planned for you!

Spectacular Idea.

Praise dance to God?

☐ hip hop ☐ jazz ☐ ballet ☐ _____ (other)

Doodle the outfit you'd wear.

Practice your dance moves right now.
Ask a friend to record your dance.
Save it on your computer or phone.

Am I now trying to win the approval of human beings, or of God? Or am I trying to please people? If I were still trying to please people, I would not be a servant of Christ.

Galatians 1:10

Make a list of people-pleaser actions. Cross each out and write a Jesus-pleaser action.

Spectacular. Idea.

Four peeps you see every day? Doodle 'em.

Label each one (fam, friend, teacher, neighbor, etc.).
    You with that person—I follow the rules, show respect, or be responsible. Cool. Tag the pic with "pleases Jesus."
    I do things 'cuz he or she wants me to. Ummm. Tag the pic with "pleases people."

8 SERIOUSLY?
LET ME SEE THAT!

When I consider your heavens, the work of your fingers, the moon and the stars, which you have set in place, what is mankind that you are mindful of them, human beings that you care for them?

Psalm 8:3–4

What is one way God (maker of the awesome sky) shows his awesome care and love for you?

Spectacular Idea.

What sky makes you feel closest to God?

starry night   fluffy clouds   snow time

mighty lightning   sparkly sunshine

Doodle it

Dear God,
When I see _____ (kind of sky) I feel so
close to you. Help me remember that you are close
to me always, not just when I am thinking about it.
Amen

9 SERIOUSLY? LET ME SEE THAT!

"Whenever the rainbow appears in the clouds, I will see it and remember the everlasting covenant between God and all living creatures of every kind on the earth."

Genesis 9:16

Pretty, pretty promise! Doodle a rainbow across both pages.

Spectacular.Idea.

Suppose *you* made a pinky promise *to Jesus*. This is just between you and God. He knows your heart. What kind of promise would you make?

- to start doing something — What?

_____

- to stop doing something — What?

_____

- to do more of something — What?

_____

Write it on the rainbow. Color it. Make it beautiful. It is a promise to God!

10 SERIOUSLY? LET ME SEE THAT!

The LORD looks down from heaven on all mankind to see if there are any who understand, any who seek God.

Psalm 14:2

Ever feel like you're trying to follow Jesus? All. By. Yourself. He sees that you are following. Uh-huh ... **he knows**. Jot down all the things that God knows.

Spectacular. Idea.

It is wise to seek God. Doodle one way you seek God.

Wisest way you follow God:
_____

Way you want to follow him:
_____

Way you want to seek him more:
_____

SERIOUSLY?
LET ME SEE THAT!

She speaks with wisdom, and faithful instruction is on her tongue.

Proverbs 31:26

Smart Talk

Spectacular. Idea.

Jot all the things you talk to Jesus about.

Are you smart-talking for God?

Fave peeps to talk to? Tape their pictures here. Write all the wise things you talk about to your faves.

12 SERIOUSLY?
LET ME SEE THAT!

Now faith is confidence in what we hope for and assurance about what we do not see. By faith we understand that the universe was formed at God's command, so that what is seen was not made out of what was visible.

Hebrews 11:1, 3

Read some awesome examples of faith in Hebrews 11! Who is your favorite? Why?

Spectacular. Idea.

God's most awesome creation?

Doodle it here.

Faith is believing ... believing that God made the world, believing that the Bible is true, believing that God has a wonderful plan for your life.

SERIOUSLY?
LET ME SEE THAT!

And now, Israel, what does the LORD your God ask of you but to fear the LORD your God, to walk in obedience to him, to love him, to serve the LORD your God with all your heart and with all your soul?

Deuteronomy 10:12

Spectacular.Idea.

walk in obedience to him …
Doodle it here.

serve the Lord
your God with
all your heart
and with all
your soul …

love him …

14 SERIOUSLY?
LET ME SEE THAT!

For you created my inmost being; you knit me together in my mother's womb. I praise you because I am fearfully and wonderfully made; your works are wonderful, I know that full well.

Psalm 139:13–14

Doodle or glue baby pic of Y-O-U.

Who has known you this whole time (baby till now)? Make a list.

Spectacular.Idea.

Is God on your list? God has known you forever. Even before you were born. In fact, he created you! Sweet!

Dear God,
The Bible says that I am _____ and _____ made. It also says that your works are _____. That is so _____. (Amazing? Awesome? Incredible? What would you say???)
Amen

15

SERIOUSLY? LET ME SEE THAT!

She opens her arms to the poor and extends her hands to the needy.

Proverbs 31:20

Read more about the kind of woman God wants you to be in Proverbs 31:10 – 31. (You are growing up, you know!)

Suppose someone at school or church is needy. How would you feel about giving something to that person?

♡ very comfortable   ♡ comfortable

♡ uncomfortable

Jesus helps those in need—even you!

Spectacular. Idea.

Suppose you could buy a gift for a child who has nothing. What would you buy? Doodle it here.

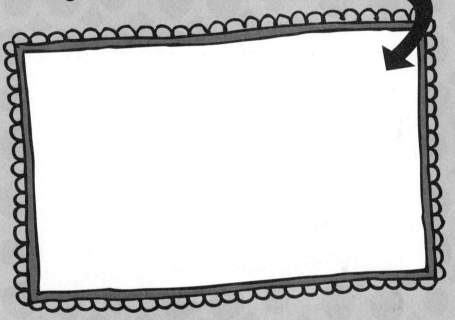

People need things, but they also need friends and help with difficult things like schoolwork. Look for chances to give today. Each time you do, draw a hand here.

16 SERIOUSLY? LET ME SEE THAT!

"I am the vine; you are the branches. If you remain in me and I in you, you will bear much fruit; apart from me you can do nothing."

John 15:5

Dear God,
[Tell him the fruit you want to see grow in your life. Hint: How do you want to be more like him?]

Please cut out the stuff that will keep me from growing.
Amen

Spectacular. Idea.

R U growing in Jesus? What fruit (proof of God in your life) are you seeing? How are you growing in him? Doodle ways UR growing in Jesus here.

17 SERIOUSLY? LET ME SEE THAT!

"I the LORD do not change."
Malachi 3:6

God created the world. Yep. So he was around when your grandma was your age. Today the same God hears your prayers!

What do you think your grandma prayed about as a girl?	What do you pray about?

Spectacular. Idea.

Glue a pic here of your grandma or a grandma-aged Christian you know. Or doodle it. (Have a pic of you together? Sweet!)

Dear God,
I want to pray all the way through my life ...
Amen

18 SERIOUSLY? LET ME SEE THAT!

So she [Rahab] let them down by a rope through the window, for the house she lived in was part of the city wall.

Joshua 2:15

Read more about Rahab the spy girl in Joshua 2! Doodle the scene here.

Joshua sent spies to look over the city of Jericho. Rahab helped the spies.

Spectacular. Idea.

I am a:

☐ spy girl (I do things behind the scenes to spread the Word of God).

☐ cheer gal (I lead others in praise joyfully out loud).

☐ comfort chick (I care for those who are hurting).

☐ serving sis (I work to meet physical needs—like food and water).

19

SERIOUSLY? LET ME SEE THAT!

Unafraid

> Keep me safe, my God,
> for in you I take refuge.
>
> *Psalm 16:1*

What were you afraid of when you were little?

Those scary things ... can stay with us. Sometimes there are some new ones too. Being safe? That is what God is all about. He is always there. ALWAYS!

Spectacular. Idea.

When is a time your heart calls to God for safety?
Doodle inside the letters and jot your fears below.
Now take a big black marker and write "SAFE IN
GOD" over each fear.

Keep me safe, God!

FEARS

SERIOUSLY?
LET ME SEE THAT!

I will praise the LORD, who counsels me.

Psalm 16:7

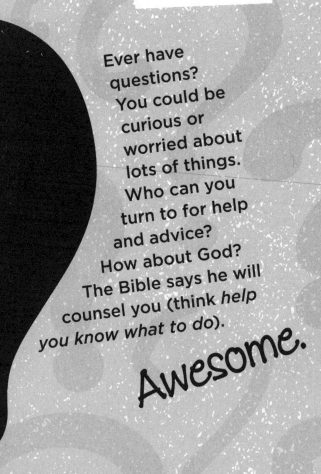

Ever have questions? You could be curious or worried about lots of things. Who can you turn to for help and advice? How about God? The Bible says he will counsel you (think *help you know what to do*).

Awesome.

Spectacular. Idea.

Doodle a couple of your questions. P-R-A-Y and wait for God's counsel. Then jot the answers to your prayers.

Oops!

Uh-oh!

SERIOUSLY?
LET ME SEE THAT!

All have sinned and fall short of the glory of God.

Romans 3:23

My bad.

Oh, no!

My goof-ups?

like most peep

tons

not too many

A goof-up I want to forget?
(Just think here … no need
to doodle it.)

Spectacular. Idea.

K. People make mistakes. Every day.

Good news! If you are a Christian, Jesus already forgot that goof-up.

No one can be perfect like Jesus. That is why God sent Jesus to pay for our sins. Don't stress!

Doodle a cross here.

Dear God,
I know that I am not perfect. I confess my goof-ups to you:
Sometimes I feel _____ because of that.
Thanks for knowing me so well and loving me so much that you sent Jesus.
Amen

22

SERIOUSLY?
LET ME SEE THAT!

In him we have redemption through his blood, the forgiveness of sins, in accordance with the riches of God's grace that he lavished on us.

Ephesians 1:7–8

Think the best gift you ever got. Glue wrapping paper around the edges of these pages.

N-O-W imagine something so much better. God wants to give you forgiveness of your sins. If you accept it, you can have eternal life with him in heaven. That "so much better" gift is called **grace**.

Spectacular.Idea.

Hey! If you ask God to forgive you of your sins, he will. He will "lavish" grace on you (think *give you more and more and more*). So how do you look with all that love and forgiveness? Glue a pic of yourself or doodle it. Surround it with beautiful wrapping paper.

SERIOUSLY?
LET ME SEE THAT!

"... Only Jesus was left, with the woman still standing there. Jesus straightened up and asked her, 'Woman, where are they? Has no one condemned you?'

'No one, sir,' she said.

'Then neither do I condemn you,' Jesus declared. 'Go now and leave your life of sin.'"

John 8:9–11

Read more in John 8! Jesus is in the business of making over girls' hearts and habits.

You can live Jesus' way as the new U.

Spectacular. Idea.

Makeover time!
I would like to make over my attitude about:

☐ school

☐ church

☐ siblings

☐ parents

☐ God

☐ my appearance

☐ other: _____

Why? What could Jesus do to makeover your heart?

_____

_____

_____

24

SERIOUSLY? LET ME SEE THAT!

be glad

> But may the righteous be glad and rejoice before God; may they be happy and joyful.
>
> Psalm 68:3

Think of how much you love God. Think of all the good things God has done for you. Doodle all those awesome things here.

Spectacular. Idea.

How many times can you write *joy* across this page? Write as tiny or as big as you want. Use different colors. Jot the number of "joys" you wrote here _____.

SERIOUSLY?
LET ME SEE THAT!

He [Jesus] will turn the hearts of the parents to their children, and the hearts of the children to their parents.

Malachi 4:6

Sometimes parents and daughters do not see things the same. Wait! When parents and daughters seek to follow Jesus, their hearts turn. They start to see more things the same.

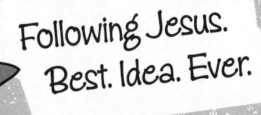

Following Jesus.
Best. Idea. Ever.

Spectacular. Idea.

What do you love about your mom or dad? Doodle it.

What does your mom or dad love about you?
(Ask them to write it here.)

Things that you both love about God.

1.
2.
3.

26

SERIOUSLY?
LET ME SEE THAT!

So I say, walk by the Spirit ... you are not to do whatever you want.

Galatians 5:16–17

Things happenin' in your life? Write about it.

Spectacular. Idea.

Doodle all the things you
do however you want.

Doodle all the things you do
by walking in the Spirit (think
following God's ways).

SERIOUSLY?
LET ME SEE THAT!

"Again I tell you, it is easier for a camel to go through the eye of a needle than for someone who is rich to enter the kingdom of God."

Matthew 19:24

not gonna happen

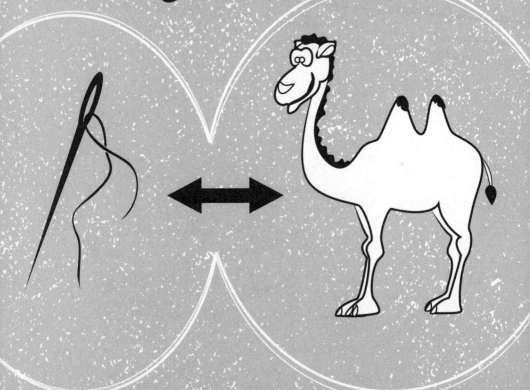

Why can things (riches) make following God like a camel trying to go through the eye of a needle?

$ People can focus on things and forget about God.

$ Things can take lots of money that could be for God's work.

$ People might work to get more things, instead of serving God.

$ _____
_____

Spectacular.Idea.

Doodle all your riches (think *any stuff you own*).

How I will use my riches to honor God:

_____
_____

28 SERIOUSLY? LET ME SEE THAT!

When you lie down, you will not be afraid; when you lie down, your sleep will be sweet.

Proverbs 3:24

You can rest your head and sleep. God has everything under control. Sweet dreams!

Glue a pic of your room here (or draw it).

Spectacular. Idea.

Probs that mess with your sleep?
Tell Jesus about it.

29

SERIOUSLY? LET ME SEE THAT!

For the entire law is fulfilled in keeping this one command: "Love your neighbor as yourself." If you bite and devour each other, watch out or you will be destroyed by each other.

Galatians 5:14–15

Spectacular. Idea.

How Jesus loves me

How I can love others

Watch out for …

Dear God,
I want to be sayin' right words when I talk about others. Help me remember to think if I would want someone to say that about me. Please help me think of words that *show love*, not *bite*, *devour*, or *destroy*. Thanks! Amen

30

SERIOUSLY?
LET ME SEE THAT!

A happy heart makes the face cheerful.

Proverbs 15:13

How does your face look?

smile

with the besties

book time
(think *homework*)

remembering
vacay

cleaning my room

Spectacular. Idea.

Knowing Jesus makes a happy heart-face. Take a pic of your happiest heart-face and tape it here.

tape here

What about knowing Jesus makes you smile?

SERIOUSLY?
LET ME SEE THAT!

But the fruit of the Spirit is love, joy, peace, forbearance, kindness, goodness, faithfulness, gentleness and self-control. Against such things there is no law.

Galatians 5:22–23

How healthy R U?
Doodle your ...

fave fruit

fave veggie

fave kind of exercise

hours of sleep a night

Spectacular. Idea.

How spiritually healthy R U? Which fruit (love, joy, peace, forbearance, kindness, goodness, faithfulness, gentleness or self-control) do your besties see in yur life?

These fruits are always in season ... and living them out is never against the rules.

32

SERIOUSLY?
LET ME SEE THAT!

Then the LORD said to Moses, "Tell Aaron, 'Stretch out your staff and strike the dust of the ground,' and throughout the land of Egypt the dust will become gnats."

Exodus 8:16

God wanted Pharaoh to let his people go, but Pharaoh was not listening. So God sent a plague (think *a very bad thing*) of a lot of gnats. *Ewww!* God wants your attention too. He isn't sending gnats to cover everything, but he is nudging your heart. What is he telling YOU to do?

Spectacular. Idea.

Doodle a place you go. What does God want YOU to do there?

33

SERIOUSLY? LET ME SEE THAT!

I am astonished that you are so quickly deserting the one who called you to live in the grace of Christ and are turning to a different gospel.

Galatians 1:6

Imagine how God feels when one of his followers turns her back on him! Lots of things can grab our attention (like popularity, sports, fashion).

Something that TRIES to be your "gospel" (first in your life): _____

Something you moved to second place to follow the gospel of Jesus: _____

Spectacular. Idea.

Pic time! Here is a picture of me following the gospel of Jesus ...
Glue or doodle pic here.

How do you follow the gospel of Jesus?

34

SERIOUSLY? LET ME SEE THAT!

I am your servant; give me discernment that I may understand your statutes.

Psalm 119:125

R U confused about anything?
Doodle your confused face.

CONFUSION???

Mark up the chart ...

	lots of ???	some ???	learning but OK
about the Bible			
about Jesus			
about becoming a Christian			
about how to live for Jesus			

Spectacular.Idea.

If you are confused about living Jesus' way, you can do these things:

1. **Talk to adult Christians.**
2. **Pray. Ask God to help you understand.**
3. **Read your Bible.**
4. **Keep reading this book.**

35

SERIOUSLY?
LET ME SEE THAT!

Yet to all who did receive him, to those who believed in his name, he gave the right to become children of God ... born of God.

John 1:12–13

The Bible says you are God's child.

Pretty amazing!

How does that happen? First, believe in God. Ask him to forgive your sins. Then you are his child. Oh yeah, you have lots of sisters.

It is a BIG, happy fam!

Spectacular.Idea.

my sisters
(or cousins or brothers)
in my family

my sisters in Jesus
(in God's family)

Hey! You are a lot like your sis!
How you are like the sis who lives at your house ...

_____ , _____ , _____

How you are like a sis in Jesus ...

_____ , _____ , _____

36

SERIOUSLY?
LET ME SEE THAT!

"And do not swear by your head, for you cannot make even one hair white or black. All you need to say is simply 'Yes' or 'No.'"

Matthew 5:36–37

Why people swear ...

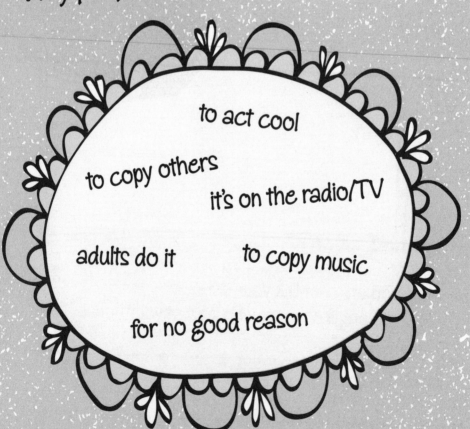

to act cool

to copy others

it's on the radio/TV

adults do it

to copy music

for no good reason

yes

no

Swearing also means to promise.
Do u ever make promises? Why?

Spectacular. Idea.

What has Jesus asked you to say yes to?
Doodle it here.

37

SERIOUSLY? LET ME SEE THAT!

"Therefore everyone who hears these words of mine and puts them into practice is like a wise man who built his house on the rock ... But everyone who hears these words of mine and does not put them into practice is like a foolish man who built his house on sand. The rain came down, the streams rose, and the winds blew and beat against that house, and it fell with a great crash."

Matthew 7:24, 26–27

Doodle a sand castle here.
Make it sparkly. Sprinkle
some sugar or glitter on it.

Fave sand castle bling?

△ shiny shells

○ colorful pebbles

□ coins

◇ gems & jewels

Now blow gently on the page. Where is the
"sparkly sand"? Doesn't take much for it to
blow away, does it?

Spectacular. Idea.

Jesus wants you to build on his words. Make a
foundation of rocks at the bottom of the page.
Write one word about Jesus' teaching on each
of the rocks.

38 SERIOUSLY? LET ME SEE THAT!

Sing and make music from your heart to the Lord, always giving thanks to God the Father for everything, in the name of our Lord Jesus Christ.

Ephesians 5:19–20

Spectacular. Idea.

Draw or paint ...

Food **MOST** thankful for

Weather **MOST** thankful for

Animal MOST thankful for

Person MOST thankful for

Dear God,
You are amazing.
Thank you for creating
so many important things, like ...

_____.

Thanks for awesome things, like ...

_____

and little cute things, like ...

_____!

_____

Amen

These things are fine, but what should you be thankful for
_____ (Hint: see verse.)

39

SERIOUSLY? LET ME SEE THAT!

"Again, truly I tell you that if two of you on earth agree about anything they ask for, it will be done for them by my Father in heaven. For where two or three gather in my name, there am I with them."

Matthew 18:19–20

Your hearts will already know what to ask if you are close to him.

Spectacular. Idea.

Plan a Jesus party! Invite 2 or 3 of your friends in Jesus. What will you do at the party? (You could praise Jesus, read his Word, pray, and plan ways to show his love to others.)

Plan It!

music:

Jesus activities:

fun:

decs:

eats:

40 SERIOUSLY?
LET ME SEE THAT!

I will tell of the kindnesses of the Lord, the deeds for which he is to be praised, according to all the Lord has done for us.

Isaiah 63:7

Spectacular.Idea.

Tell about God's kindness to you ...
(Grab a white or silver marker or crayon.)

God has been kind by providing what I need.

God has been kind by giving me talents.

God has been kind in sending Jesus.

God has been kind in my relationships.

Doodle a mini PRAISE poster here:

SERIOUSLY?
LET ME SEE THAT!

"Love your neighbor as yourself."
Matthew 22:39

Where's your neighbor?

next chair
at dinner ...

next house
over ...

next desk
at school ...

next seat
on the bus …

in another
town …

all over
the world …

Spectacular. Idea.
How can you love your neighbor? Doodle it here.

42 SERIOUSLY? LET ME SEE THAT!

For God so loved the world that he gave his one and only Son, that whoever believes in him shall not perish but have eternal life.

John 3:16

What *do* people mean when they say they are Christians? Here it is:

(1) Everybody makes mistakes. (We are all sinners.)

(2) Believe that God sent his Son, Jesus, to die for our sins.

(3) Ask Jesus to be the Lord (in charge) of your life.

Okay. So becoming a Christian happens in your heart. Tell about it ...

Important peeps in my life!

☐ fam   ☐ friends   ☐ teachers

☐ _____ (other)

Yep. Being a Christian. It's important for all of them too.

SERIOUSLY?
LET ME SEE THAT!

run, baby, run

Do you not know that in a race all the runners run, but only one gets the prize? Run in such a way as to get the prize.

1 Corinthians 9:24

Being a Christian is kind of like running (think *cross country or jogging*). You warm up (learn about Jesus); you practice (live your faith); and you reach the prize (eternal life).

Spectacular. Idea.

Running shoes? Make them your own: colors, stripes, stars, neon, glow in the dark...

Wearing the right shoes helps you run the race. Your spiritual shoes? Doodle 'em. Tell about 'em.

44 SERIOUSLY? LET ME SEE THAT!

"You have heard that it was said, 'Love your neighbor and hate your enemy.' But I tell you, love your enemies and pray for those who persecute you"

Matthew 5:43–44

Being nice to hard-to-be-nice-to peeps ...
What might happen? Doodle it.

Sorry you were sick! I can show you what we learned in math.

Spectacular. Idea.

Some peeps I know ...

← easy to be nice to | hard to be nice to →

easy to be nice to	hard to be nice to
_____	_____
_____	_____
_____	_____
_____	_____
_____	_____
_____	_____

how can I show everyone love?

_____

SERIOUSLY?
LET ME SEE THAT!

Therefore my people will know my name.

Isaiah 52:6

Spectacular. Idea.

Doodle one of the names for God.

If you are telling your BFF about God, what words could describe God? Doodle those words (think beautiful bold letters for the words *love* or *awesome*).

I call on God's name:

- [ ] lots
- [ ] before I eat
- [ ] at bedtime
- [ ] on Sundays
- [ ] when I have a prob
- [ ] not too much

You know his name.
Call. on. it. lots.

46

SERIOUSLY?
LET ME SEE THAT!

For by one sacrifice he has made perfect forever those who are being made holy.

Hebrews 10:14

Have you ever wanted a new look?

A makeover might be fun, but the Bible talks about a makeover of the heart. It is the best kind of beauty. It never goes out of style.

Spectacular. Idea.

My New Look
(for fun)

My New Heart
(for forever)

Love, love, love it!

47

SERIOUSLY?
LET ME SEE THAT!

"And if anyone gives even a cup of cold water to one of these little ones who is my disciple, truly I tell you, that person will certainly not lose their reward."

Matthew 10:42

What else did Jesus say about this idea?
Read Matthew 10:40–42!

Spectacular. Idea.

Giving water shows Jesus' love and caring. You can give other things that people need too. Grab a few magazines and cut out pics of what YOU could give. Glue or tape here. Or doodle your own collage.

Jesus cares about our physical needs. He cares about our heart needs too. What do you need right now? _____
Pray about it. He is listening.

48

SERIOUSLY?
LET ME SEE THAT!

Offer hospitality to one another without grumbling.

1 Peter 4:9

Think of putting the needs of others first. That's what hospitality really is—much more than being a good hostess.

Spectacular. Idea.

Pick one! Doodle it!

- ☐ Your sis has a friend staying all night. Sis wants the friend to have your bed.
- ☐ Your mom has a meeting at your house. One lady brings her little girl who loves *your* fave snack.
- ☐ Your friend comes to visit. She asks to use your special glitter markers.

Tell of a time when someone showed Jesus' kind of hospitality to you.

49

SERIOUSLY?
LET ME SEE THAT!

I no longer call you servants, because a servant does not know his master's business. Instead, I have called you friends, for everything that I learned from my Father I have made known to you.

John 15:15

Doodle it! Someone asks about Jesus.
What ya gonna say?

Rate it!
A friend asks you about Jesus.

- ☐ easy to talk about
- ☐ subject change!

You pray it won't rain on the picnic. It doesn't.

- ☐ give Jesus the credit
- ☐ say you were lucky

You don't swear.

- ☐ blame it on parent rules
- ☐ say you try to follow Jesus

Spectacular. Idea.

Jesus. Proud 2 know U. The best friend a girl will EVER have.

50

SERIOUSLY?
LET ME SEE THAT!

Then he said to his disciples, "The harvest is plentiful but the workers are few. Ask the Lord of the harvest, therefore, to send out workers into his harvest field."

Matthew 9:37–38

Willing to help gather people to Jesus?

definitely

not ready

maybe

Spectacular. Idea.

How could you show your friends the way to Jesus? Doodle it.

Jesus will show YOU how to show OTHERS the way. Just ask him.

Dear God,
I want to be one of your workers. Today I'm praying about _____, _____, and _____. Please show me how to lead them to you.
Amen

51

SERIOUSLY?
LET ME SEE THAT!

Charm is deceptive, and beauty is fleeting; but a woman who fears the LORD is to be praised.

Proverbs 31:30

Spectacular. Idea.

How-do-I-look beauty takes time. Relationship-with-Jesus beauty takes time too. How will you work on your relationship-with-Jesus beauty? Doodle three ideas.

Name someone you know who has relationship-with-Jesus beauty: _____.

52

SERIOUSLY?
LET ME SEE THAT!

List my tears on your scroll.

Psalm 56:8

Sometimes your heart can be so sad. Tears? They happen. Good news! Jesus is listening. He knows when your heart is sad. He even has a list of your tears.

Spectacular. Idea.

Every tear? Jesus has a list.
Your tear list?

teeny tiny _____

small _____

medium _____

big _____

HUGE _____

53

SERIOUSLY? LET ME SEE THAT!

"You shall have no other gods before me."

Exodus 20:3

Rate 'em. Where is your heart?
Be honest! Tell your heart!

PEOPLE

not important   kind of important   very important!

POPULARITY

not important   kind of important   very important!

CLOTHES

not important   kind of important   very important!

MONEY

not important   kind of important   very important!

POSSESSIONS

not important   kind of important   very important!

ACTIVITIES

not important   kind of important   very important!

Spectacular. Idea.

Okay. Now how does God rate in your heart?

_____

Dear God,
I did a heart check. It looks like I need to put
_____ and _____ (things) in their
place. I want you to have first place in all the parts
of my heart.
Amen

54

SERIOUSLY?
LET ME SEE THAT!

All the ends of the earth will remember and turn to the Lord, and all the families of the nations will bow down before him.

Psalm 22:27

Bowing to God?

A sign of our worship, love, and following.

Doodle a few different types of bows.

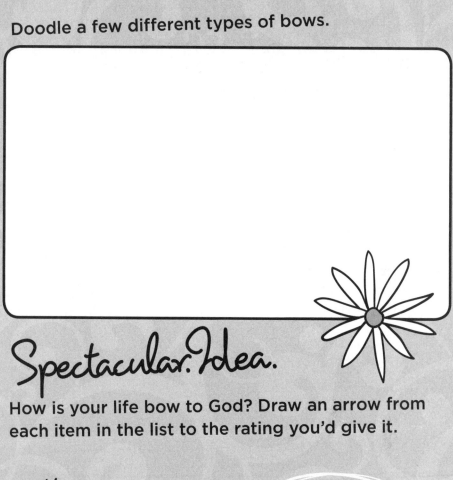

Spectacular. Idea.

How is your life bow to God? Draw an arrow from each item in the list to the rating you'd give it.

at home

um, not really
bowing

at school

in stores

so-so
bow

at the movies

fantastic
bow

on the sports field

55

SERIOUSLY? LET ME SEE THAT!

> "You shall not give false testimony against your neighbor."
>
> *Exodus 20:16*

Five things that are true	Five things that are false
1.	1.
2.	2.
3.	3.
4.	4.
5.	5.

Tell the truth? You ...

	for sure	it depends	prob not	never
see cheating	☐	☐	☐	☐
break a rule	☐	☐	☐	☐
get a bad grade	☐	☐	☐	☐
notice stealing	☐	☐	☐	☐

Spectacular. Idea.

Pick one of the above situations. Doodle how you could handle the truth God's way.

56

SERIOUSLY?
LET ME SEE THAT!

> "Remember the Sabbath day by keeping it holy. Six days you shall labor and do all your work, but the seventh day is a sabbath to the Lord your God. On it you shall not do any work."
>
> *Exodus 20:8–10*

Spectacular. Idea.

Suppose you get a Save the Date card from Jesus. What does he want you to save Sunday for?

How are you gonna keep Sunday free? Turn the book sideways and make a plan for each day this week!

MONDAY	TUESDAY	WEDNESDAY	THURSDAY	FRIDAY	SATURDAY	SUNDAY
						No Work
						Keep it holy.

57

SERIOUSLY?
LET ME SEE THAT!

"Honor your father and your mother."
Exodus 20:12

I will honor my parents because:

1. It is God's commandment.

2. _____

3. _____

Spectacular. Idea.

Cheese! Time to get your parents' pics. Glue them here or doodle them.

Your mom and dad have known you a long time. The only one who has known you longer is God. (He knew you before you were born. In fact, he knew that you would be born long, long ago.)

58

SERIOUSLY?
LET ME SEE THAT!

Jesus said:
"You have heard that it was said to the people long ago, 'You shall not murder, and anyone who murders will be subject to judgment.' But I tell you that anyone who is angry with a brother or sister will be subject to judgment."

Matthew 5:21–22

chill

Spectacular. Idea.

So you need to chill, even when someone upsets you. Doodle or write inside the cube.

If my best friend tells my secret, I will ...

If the girls gossip about me, I will ...

When my little sis drops my fave ring down the toilet, I will ...

Doodle ways you can chill.

59

SERIOUSLY? LET ME SEE THAT!

> "When the Son of Man comes in his glory, and all the angels with him, he will sit on his glorious throne. All the nations will be gathered before him."
>
> Matthew 25:31–32

Read the verses again. How will it be when Jesus returns? Doodle it. Bling out his crown.

You know royalty! Jesus is the Prince of Peace. He is coming back to the earth. He will rule as King.

Spectacular. Idea.

Best time to tell others about Jesus? (circle)

now

when he returns

Ways to tell about Jesus?
(Circle the ones you could do.)

tell what he means to me

invite to church

write a note

give a Bible

send a text

give a Christian CD

give a book about him

show his love

_____ (what else?)

60 SERIOUSLY?
LET ME SEE THAT!

"You shall not steal."

Exodus 20:15

You would never hold up a bank or take something that belongs to a friend. Are there other kinds of stealing? Yep. Not yours? Don't take it.

Spectacular. Idea.

Situation #1 At the library. You really want to check out the newest book on fashion. You are going on vacay tomorrow. The sign says new books can't be checked out for two weeks. Jot yur thots.

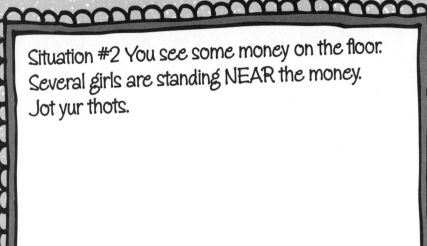

Situation #2 You see some money on the floor. Several girls are standing NEAR the money. Jot yur thots.

Situation #3 Everyone has gone home. Someone left a fab pen on the table. Jot yur thots.

SERIOUSLY?
LET ME SEE THAT!

"Moses said to the people, "Do not be afraid.
God has come to test you, so that the fear of
God will be with you to keep you from sinning.'"

Exodus 20:20

There are **10** Commandments.

Quick, can you list them all?

(Turn to Exodus 20 for help.)

1. _____

2. _____

3. _____

4. _____

5. _____

6. _____

7. _____

8. _____

9. _____

10. _____

No prob. _____

Spectacular. Idea.

Doodle a symbol for each commandment
that will help you remember all 10.

62

SERIOUSLY? LET ME SEE THAT!

"You shall not covet your neighbor's house ... or anything that belongs to your neighbor."

Exodus 20:17

"Covet" means ... wanting something that is not yours. It's just plain jelly. Don't. Do. That. K?

Suppose you really think about it ...

I ❤ _____ (something that is NOT yours)

What could fill in the blank?

○ cool clothes

○ a huge house

○ a beautiful bod

○ popular friends

Doodle all the ways your eyes look when you really, really wish you had someone else's stuff.

Spectacular. Idea.

Then doodle how your eyes look when you are happy for someone else. Pair them up with a mouth if you wish. Don't forget the eyebrows!

63

SERIOUSLY?
LET ME SEE THAT!

And he will be called Wonderful Counselor, Mighty God, Everlasting Father, Prince of Peace.

Isaiah 9:6

Ever heard someone say, "Peace"? What does that really mean? No fighting. No worries. Calm. Trust. "Peace" is an expression, but Christians know the Prince of Peace.

Spectacular. Idea.

A time when Jesus gave you peace? Doodle it.

A time when you need Jesus' peace? Doodle it.

Dear God,
I get worried and upset (pick one)
○ every day   ○ once in a while   ○ almost never.
When that happens, I need your kind of peace.
Okay. I need you in my life. Every. Single. Day.
Amen

64

SERIOUSLY?
LET ME SEE THAT!

When they saw the star, they were overjoyed. On coming to the house, they saw the child with his mother Mary, and they bowed down and worshiped him.

Matthew 2:10–11

That amazing star led the magi (wise men) to the baby Jesus. Why did they follow it? They wanted to worship the baby King.

It is fun to look at the stars. Sometimes you can even find the shape a group of stars makes, called a constellation. Doodle your own constellation.

Spectacular. Idea.

Fast forward to today. Suppose that YOU were traveling to worship the baby King Jesus. What would you take? Doodle it here. Show how you would worship him.

65 SERIOUSLY? LET ME SEE THAT!

Provide purses for yourselves that will not wear out, a treasure in heaven that will never fail, where no thief comes near and no moth destroys. For where your treasure is, there your heart will be also.

Luke 12:33–34

Do you have a purse you love, love, love? (Doodle it ... and the stuff inside.)

Spectacular. Idea.

Do you have a purse that will NEVER wear out?
(Hint: your heart with God's promises inside)
Doodle it and add some of your fave Bible promises.

Bible math: your treasure
(things you love) = where your
heart is.

A question:
Where is **your** treasure?

66 SERIOUSLY? LET ME SEE THAT!

"All these people gave their gifts out of their wealth; but she out of her poverty put in all she had to live on."

Luke 21:4

You can read the widow's story in Luke 21:1—4

Is there something you don't have much of?

- ☐ money
- ☐ time
- ☐ friends
- ☐ grades
- ☐ clothes
- ☐ influence (Do people listen to you?)
- ☐ authority (Do you make the rules or important decisions?)

Spectacular Idea.

Look for ways you can give to Jesus today (even in small ways). Each time you find one add two coins to the piggy bank.

Dear God,
I am _____ (insert age). That means I don't have much _____ to offer you, but I will give all that I have today.
Amen

67

SERIOUSLY?
LET ME SEE THAT!

When they kept on questioning him, he straightened up and said to them, "Let any one of you who is without sin be the first to throw a stone at her."

John 8:7

Read more about what Jesus said about throwing stones in John 8:7 – 11.

What are some "rocks" that people throw today? Write them in the rocks.

unkind words

ignoring

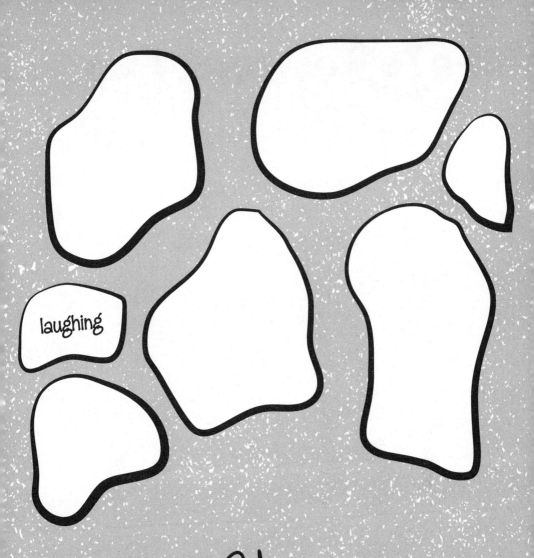

68 SERIOUSLY? LET ME SEE THAT!

> *"And even the very hairs of your head are all numbered. So don't be afraid."*
>
> Matthew 10:30–31

Ever strrreeesss??? Oh yeah. God knows. All about you. He even knows the number of hairs on your head. So ... if he knows all of that ... why strrreeesss?

Your hair. Tape or
glue pics here.

Great Do

Bad Hair Day

Spectacular Idea

Dear God,
You are so amazing to know how many hairs I
have on my head! I know I can trust you to know
all the important things about my life too, like
_____ and _____. I won't be
afraid. I will trust you.
Amen

69 SERIOUSLY? LET ME SEE THAT!

"And why do you worry about clothes? See how the flowers of the field grow. They do not labor or spin. Yet I tell you that not even Solomon in all his splendor was dressed like one of these ... But seek first his kingdom and his righteousness, and all these things will be given to you as well.

Matthew 6:28–29, 33

Spectacular. Idea.

God makes beautiful flowers. He takes care of them. God made you too. He knows everything you need. He does not want you to worry, Lily! Draw, paste, or trace some of the most beautiful flowers here.

Glue a picture of your face in the center of one of those flowers. No pic? Doodle one!

70 SERIOUSLY?
LET ME SEE THAT!

> I have learned the secret of being content in any and every situation.... I can do all this through him who gives me strength.
>
> Philippians 4:12-13

How do you describe yourself?
Write your answers here.

BTW—did you say that you are strong?

Breathe a good sigh, the kind that means *I'm OK right now*, or *I know God is taking care of me.* Worry? Nah. Impatient? Not me. That's being content.

Rate these.

1—very content
2—doesn't matter
3—not content at all

____ late ride

____ dishwasher detail

____ in a long line

____ at practice

____ your BDay

____ homework time

____ have the flu

____ at a party

____ vacay

Spectacular. Idea.

God can make you content. He wants to make you strong in the tough or just plain annoying times. Just ask him.

71

SERIOUSLY? LET ME SEE THAT!

Devote yourselves to prayer, being watchful and thankful.

Colossians 4:2

Spectacular. Idea.

List the things this verse says about prayer.

1.

2.

3.

Now make a different kind of prayer list. List some things you will pray about. (Remember to follow the three steps above as you pray!)

1.

2.

3.

Just wonderin' … do you have a fave prayer place? Doodle it. You can pray anywhere anytime, but it is sweet to have a special place to go for prayer.

72

SERIOUSLY?
LET ME SEE THAT!

"My Father's house has many rooms; if that were not so, would I have told you that I am going there to prepare a place for you?"

John 14:2

Jesus promised to be with you every day.
He also promised to make a place for you in heaven.
You will be where God's glory shines forever.

"You are worthy, our Lord and God, to receive glory and honor and power."

Revelation 4:11

Spectacular. Idea.

What will happen in heaven?
Doodle three things God receives in heaven.

These should happen on earth too!

73

SERIOUSLY?
LET ME SEE THAT!

Today, if only you would hear his voice, "Do not harden your hearts."

Psalm 95:7–8

Soft heart? Hard heart?
Doodle around each to show
hard or soft.

Hey! What is God saying to your soft heart?

I feel sad for a friend.

I am yelling.

I give to someone in need.

I am impatient.

I explain math to a classmate.

I decide not to obey.

Spectacular. Idea.

What kind of heart do you have? Is it hard? The Bible teaches that if your heart is hard, you won't hear the voice of God. You just have to have a soft heart to hear him. Wait a minute ... God is speaking?

Yep.

Here I am ...

when my heart is hard

when my heart is soft

74

SERIOUSLY?
LET ME SEE THAT!

How beautiful on the mountains are the feet of those who bring good news, who proclaim peace, who bring good tidings, who proclaim salvation, who say to Zion, "Your God reigns!"

Isaiah 52:7

What beautiful news of God's peace and salvation! Doesn't it make your feet want to run and tell the Good News as well?

Get your feet ready to go …
a good pedicure would be fab.
Draw or trace your tootsies here.
Paint and decorate the nails.

Fun! The important thing is going—not your nails

Spectacular. Idea.

Where will **you** stand and tell others about the Good News of Jesus' peace and salvation? Circle the feet that could be yours, or fill in your own idea.

I will tell about Jesus' peace and salvation to ...

someone who is hurting

someone who is down

someone who is sick

75

SERIOUSLY?
LET ME SEE THAT!

Love is patient, love is kind. It does not envy, it does not boast, it is not proud. It does not dishonor others, it is not self-seeking, it is not easily angered, it keeps no record of wrongs. Love does not delight in evil but rejoices with the truth. It always protects, always trusts, always hopes, always perseveres.

1 Corinthians 13:4 – 7

Read more about love in the whole chapter of 1 Corinthians 13.

Doodle some things you L-O-V-E.

Do they show God's kind of love?

Spectacular. Idea.

A time you showed Bible love? Jot yur thots here.

Now draw a trail of hearts. Next to each heart,
write one way to describe Bible love.

76

SERIOUSLY?
LET ME SEE THAT!

Don't you know that you yourselves are God's temple and that God's Spirit dwells in your midst?

1 Corinthians 3:16

Spectacular. Idea.

You are God's temple. That is huge. A temple isn't just any old building. It is a place for honor, respect, and care. You are very important.

Doodle how you could make God proud ...

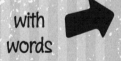

with words

with
activities

with
healthy
habits

How do you take care of God's temple?

_____

_____

_____

77

SERIOUSLY?
LET ME SEE THAT!

If any of you lacks wisdom, you should ask God, who gives generously to all without finding fault, and it will be given to you.

James 1:5

Spectacular. Idea.

Dear God,

Here is the biggest question I have—just between us. Doodle or write your question on a separate piece of paper. Fold it then tape or glue it here.

tape or glue it here

Hint:
Where does the Bible tell you to get answers?

How will God feel about your question?
Read the verse again. He will give _____.

God wants you to ask him

ANYTHING.

Dear God,
Thanks for always being there to answer my
questions about _____!
It is great to NOT be alone!
Amen

78 SERIOUSLY? LET ME SEE THAT!

Now to him who is able to do immeasurably more than all we ask or imagine, according to his power that is at work within us, to him be glory ... for ever and ever! Amen.

Ephesians 3:20–21

Need God's power? Doodle one situation where you need it now.

Sometimes it is not about God working through us. Sometimes it is about him coming into the situation and doing something amazing. Doodle one situation where you need God to come in and do something amazing.

Spectacular. Idea.

Dear God,
Either way, it is not about MY power. It is totally about YOUR power. Amazing! I really need YOUR power here:

○ school   ○ church
○ home   ○ the hood
○ friends   ○ Okay. ALL of the above.

Amen

SERIOUSLY?
LET ME SEE THAT!

She [Martha] came to him [Jesus] and said, "Lord, doesn't it seem unfair to you that my sister just sits here while I do all the work? Tell her to come and help me."

But the Lord said to her, "My dear Martha, you are worried and upset over all these details! There is only one thing worth being concerned about. Mary has discovered it, and it will not be taken away from her."

Luke 10:40–42 NLT

Spectacular. Idea.

Suppose Jesus came to **your** house and you could ask him anything ... ANYTHING! What would you give him to eat? Doodle it.

What would you say?

What would you talk about?

◯ family

◯ friends

◯ school

◯ It's private.

BTW—You CAN talk to him anytime you want. *That* is called **prayer**!

80 SERIOUSLY? LET ME SEE THAT!

"You are the salt of the earth. But if the salt loses its saltiness, how can it be made salty again? It is no longer good for anything, except to be thrown out and trampled underfoot."

Matthew 5:13

Okay. Jesus taught that his followers are salt. Hmmm. Think about salt as making something better. Think about adding Jesus' ways (thoughts, words, attitudes, reactions) to what is happening.

Spectacular. Idea.

The Bible says you are salt ... or let's say you *should be* salt ...

Your saltshaker? (pic of you)

A situation where you can add God's flavor (teachings, love, forgiveness, patience, joy)? What is on the plate? Doodle it. Add more plates.

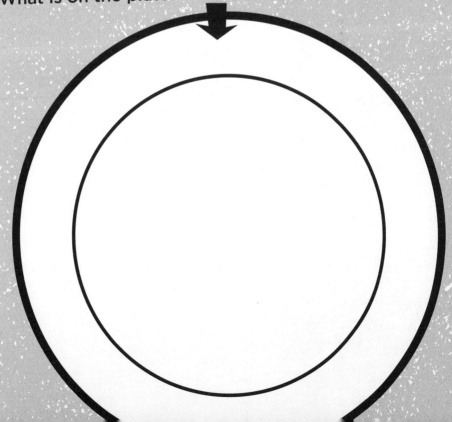

81

SERIOUSLY?
LET ME SEE THAT!

do good

Therefore, as we have opportunity, let us do good to all people, especially to those who belong to the family of believers.

Galatians 6:10

Spectacular. Idea.

When has someone done something good 4U? How did you feel?

Doodle a time you did good for someone.

It was ...
(circle one)

to another
Christian
(believer)

to someone
else

Hey! Either one is good.
Now try to "do good" to
someone in the other
group today.

God, Can I Talk to You?

Dear God,
Sometimes it's easier for me to "do good"
to (pick one) Christians /others. Will you
help me with the other group? Thanks!
Amen

82

SERIOUSLY?
LET ME SEE THAT!

Do not merely listen to the word, and so deceive yourselves. Do what it says. Anyone who listens to the word but does not do what it says is like someone who looks at his face in a mirror and, after looking at himself, goes away and immediately forgets what he looks like. But whoever looks intently into the perfect law that gives freedom, and continues in it—not forgetting what they have heard, but doing it—they will be blessed in what they do.

James 1:22-25

You and God's Word. What happens next?

1. You hear the Word, but nothing happens.

OR

2. You do more than hear. You LOOK AT (think *study*) God's Word. Then you act on what you have learned.

Spectacular Idea.

Something that you have heard
from God's Word:

How it looks when I live it:

83

SERIOUSLY?
LET ME SEE THAT!

"And who knows but that you have come to your royal position for such a time as this?"

Esther 4:14

Esther was a queen, but she was not like the others. Her fam was Jewish. So what happened when the king ordered that the Jews to be killed? Esther was able to use her position and influence to save her people.

Read more about it in the book of Esther!

Spectacular. Idea.

What is your "position" in life right now? Circle the crowns in bright colors for all that you are.

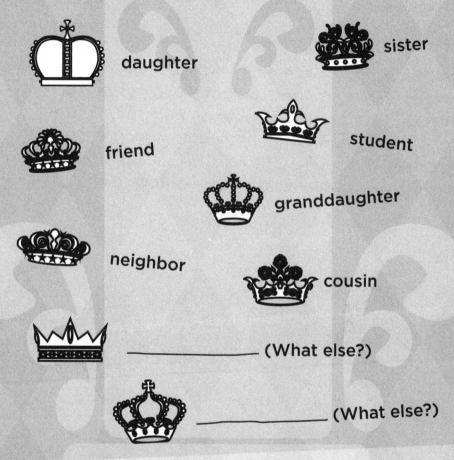

daughter

sister

friend

student

granddaughter

neighbor

cousin

_____ (What else?)

_____ (What else?)

Write about one real-life situation where God wants you to influence others right now.

84

SERIOUSLY?
LET ME SEE THAT!

She hid him for three months. But when she could hide him no longer, she got a papyrus basket for him and coated it with tar and pitch. Then she placed the child in it and put it among the reeds along the bank of the Nile. His sister stood at a distance to see what would happen to him.

Exodus 2:2–4

Talk about adventures in babysitting!
Read the whole story in Exodus 1:8–2:10.

Me? A babysitter?

sure

maybe

ewww!

When you take care of little kids, you never know what they will grow up to be.

a little kid you know

what he or she might grow up to be

This might come to pass —
you never know.

Spectacular. Idea.

God does not call everyone to babysit. What is another way you could help little kids grow in Christ? Doodle it here.

85

SERIOUSLY?
LET ME SEE THAT!

Purify me from my sins, and I will be clean; wash me, and I will be whiter than snow.

Psalm 51:7 NLT

Think of something you want to ask Jesus to forgive you for. Use a pencil to write it on this shirt.

Now erase your words. Can you kind of still see them? Borrow some whiteout from your parents and white out the words. Pretty, clean, all forgiven—that is how God sees you after you accept Jesus.

Spectacular. Idea.

Most comfy T-shirt? Doodle
it on the clothesline.

V-neck

scoop neck

tank

long-sleeved
slouch

Now doodle and white out. Jesus forgives.

86 SERIOUSLY? LET ME SEE THAT!

Let love and faithfulness never leave you; bind them around your neck, write them on the tablet of your heart. Then you will win favor and a good name in the sight of God and man.

Proverbs 3:3–4

Need an upgrade? (We ALL do!) What apps (think *habits*) would help you live more like Jesus? (Hey—look at the verses for two ideas.) Draw those apps in the app boxes below.

Spectacular. Idea.

Doodle a screenshot of your heart tablet.
Be honest, girl! Doodle it here.
Dec it out with your habits, interests, activities.

Dear God,
Everybody needs an upgrade. I need to break this
habit: _____. So I need your _____.
Amen

87

SERIOUSLY?
LET ME SEE THAT!

For I am convinced that neither death nor life, neither angels nor demons, neither the present nor the future, nor any powers, neither height nor depth, nor anything else in all creation, will be able to separate us from the love of God that is in Christ Jesus our Lord.

Romans 8:38–39

Jesus & Me

Spectacular. Idea.

Doodle some things that feel like they could separate you from God's love. Hint: Read the verse again.

Now draw a giant X through each thing.

Jesus is always with you—always. Always. **ALWAYS**. It doesn't matter where you are. He is with you. **NOTHING** can separate you from God's love.

What a beautiful promise!

88

SERIOUSLY?
LET ME SEE THAT!

"This perfume could have been sold at a high price and the money given to the poor."

Aware of this, Jesus said to them, "Why are you bothering this woman? She has done a beautiful thing to me."

Matthew 26:9-10

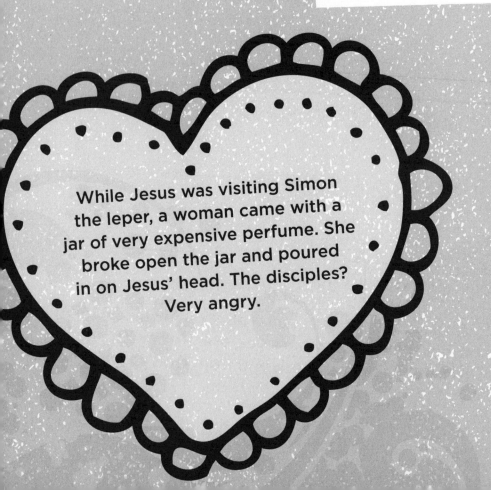

While Jesus was visiting Simon the leper, a woman came with a jar of very expensive perfume. She broke open the jar and poured in on Jesus' head. The disciples? Very angry.

Spectacular. Idea.

Glue or tape pics of your most valuable possessions here.

Something valuable you would give to Jesus?

Something you would give to the poor to show Jesus' love?

89

SERIOUSLY?
LET ME SEE THAT!

"Therefore go and make disciples of all nations, baptizing them in the name of the Father and of the Son and of the Holy Spirit, and teaching them to obey everything I have commanded you. And surely I am with you always, to the very end of the age."

Matthew 28:19–20

Spectacular. Idea.

K ... Where will you go? How will you get there? What will YOU say about Jesus?

90

SERIOUSLY?
LET ME SEE THAT!

"At that time people will see the Son of Man coming in clouds with great power and glory."

Mark 13:26

Awesome!

Why is Jesus coming back? He is coming for the believers here on earth. When? No one knows, but it's going to be fabulous.

We need to be ready.

Spectacular.Idea.

Where might you be when Jesus returns? Make a list.

Where will you go today? Pick one. Doodle it here.

Thank you for sharing your doodle talents and your faith in Jesus with us.

Dare U 2 Open This Book

Draw It, Write It, Dare 2 Live It

Carol McAdams Moore

Dare U 2 Open This Book is not your typical 90-day devotional for boys. It's an all-out open space for them to explore and learn more about themselves and their faith, using creative, wacky applications and doodle opps to teach Bible truths.

Available in stores and online!